Grand Canyon

National Park

Animals & Attractions

Billy Grinslott & Kinsey Marie Books

ISBN - 9781960612854

There are many birds, reptiles and snakes in Grand Canyon. We have listed the larger animals that may be easier to spot and fun to see from a distance.

California condors are the largest birds in North America. They have a wingspans of 10 feet and weigh over 20 pounds. The California condor is estimated to live over 60 years. They are a weird looking bird and resemble the vulture. They can fly as high as 15 thousand feet.

Bald eagles live in just about every part of the world. The largest bald eagles tend to live in Alaska where they sometimes weigh as much as 17 pounds. They build the largest nest of any North American bird. The Bald Eagle is America's national bird. They return to the same nesting area every year.

The cliff chipmunk is small, and bushy tailed. It lives along cliff walls or boulders. Their stripes and face stripes are a little different than other chipmunks. Chipmunks are small members of the squirrel family. They have pouches inside of their cheeks so they can carry food. They are very friendly and will take food from your hand.

Rock squirrels live in burrows which they dig with their sharp claws and muscular legs. Unlike other squirrels they have adapted to living in treeless areas. They will climb trees if there is any in the area. Rock squirrels are one of the largest squirrel species. They grow up to a length of around 17 to 21 inches. Squirrels are important plant dispersers. They gather seeds and nuts and bury them in the dirt, which grows new plants.

Hog-nosed Skunk live in canyons, stream sides, and rocky terrain. They are no different than other skunks. If you scare them, they will flip their tail at you and spray you with a stinky potion. American hog-nosed skunks are found from the southern United States. Hog-nosed skunks are nocturnal, they usually only come out at night. They have different color patterns than the normal skunk.

Ringtails look like a racoon. They have stripes on their tails, but their face more resembles a cat. They are a member of the racoon family. Ringtails can be found in the south and southwestern parts of America. Ringtails are excellent climbers capable of ascending vertical walls, trees, rocky cliffs and even cactus. They are mostly nocturnal.

Gray fox prefers to live in rocky canyons and ridges but can also be found in wooded areas and open fields. They have strong, hooked claws that enable them to climb trees. Which is abnormal for a dog species. Gray foxes are not observed as frequently as red foxes due to their reclusive nature and more nocturnal habits.

The coyote is bigger than a fox. Eastern coyotes are part wolf. Coyotes are great for pest control. They like to eat mice and rats. They can adapt and live almost anywhere, even in the city. They have a yip type of call when they communicate with each other. Coyotes are found in all the United States, except Hawaii.

Javelina are classified as herbivores. They eat a variety of native plants and roots. They live in groups, which helps them with survival. Baby javelinas are called reds, because when they are young their hair is a red color. They are not part of the pig family. They belong to a separate family of mammals called the collared peccary.

The mountain lion is one of the biggest cats in North America. The largest mountain lion ever recorded weighed 276 pounds. Mountain lions don't roar like other big cats they communicate in different ways, such as chirping, growling, shrieking, and even purring.

Mule deer get their name because of their mule like ears. Male deer are called bucks and females are does. Males grow new antlers every year. They can run 30 miles per hour. They are bigger than whitetail deer and prefer living in the mountain areas.

Desert Bighorn sheep are highly adapted for desert climates and can go for extended periods of time without drinking. They are social animals and form herds that are usually 8 to 10 sheep. Males will challenge each other and slam their heads together, that's how they got their name ram. Their horns can weigh up to 30 pounds.

Weighing in at up to 700 pounds, the Elk is one of the biggest deer species on earth. They can run as fast as 40 miles per hour. They can outrun horses. They make a cool bugling sound when communicating with other elk. It's fun to listen to them. Only male elk have antlers. That they shed and regrow every year.

Bison are only found on the North Rim of Grand Canyon National Park. The North American Bison and Buffalo are sometimes confused as the same animal, but they are not. Bison have long hair on their backs, front, and a long beard. Bison are bigger than buffalo. They are the largest mammal in North America and weigh up to 2,000 pounds.

These next pages will show some of the most popular sites to see and visit. At the end we will cover some activities you can do.

Grand Canyon National Park is bigger than the entire state of Rhode Island. It is 1,904 square miles in size and 1 mile deep. The South Rim is the most popular place to visit at Grand Canyon National Park. The South Rim is located in northern Arizona. The south rim offers many things to do and see. Many trails can be accessed from the South rim.

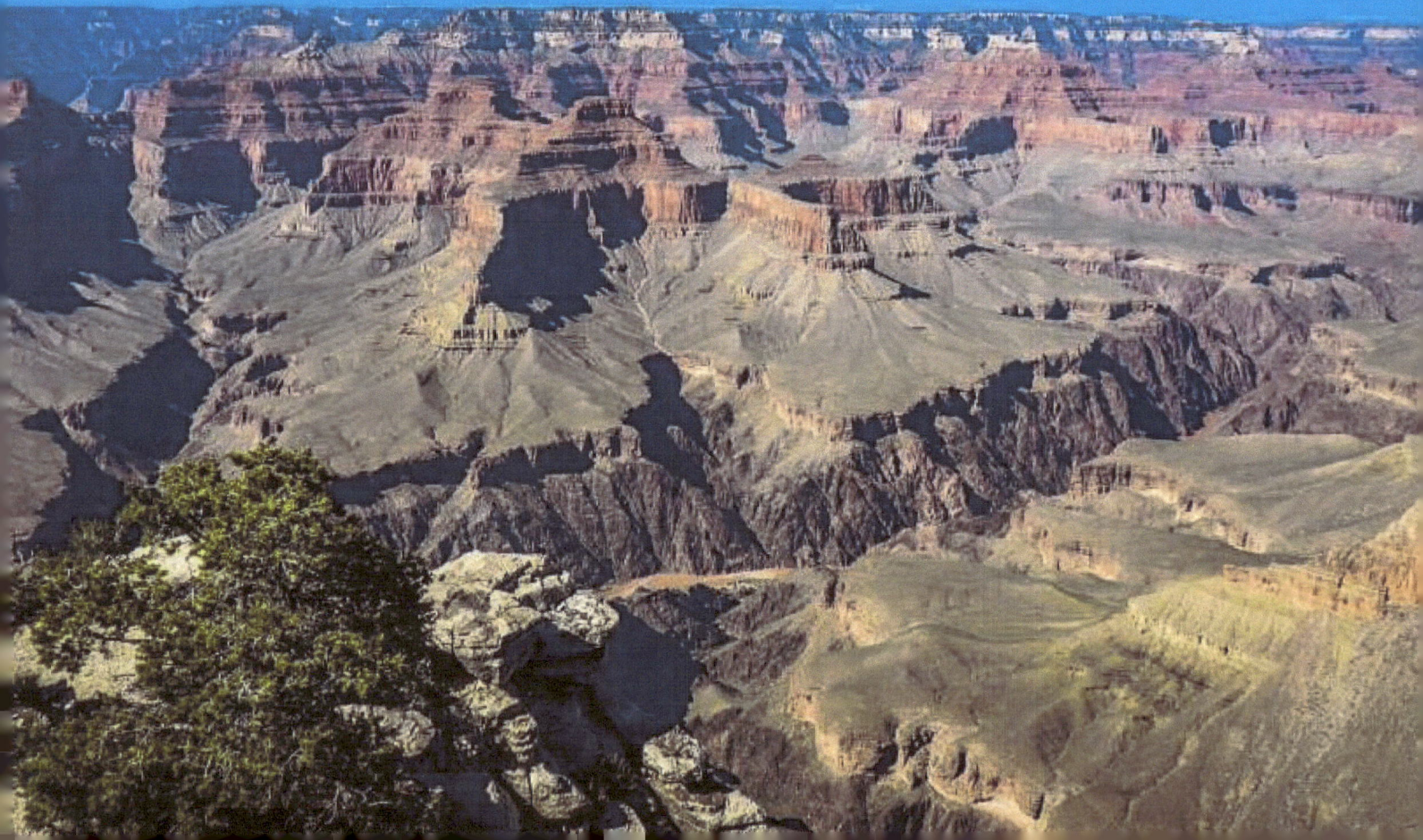

Bright Angel Trail is considered the most popular hiking trail in the park. It is fairly easy to walk down. This can be a blessing or a curse. You will enjoy wide views of the inner canyon and distant formations. The return hike back up and out of the canyon is far more difficult and requires much more effort. It will take you to some tunnels and resting places. The total length is 12 miles roundtrip, but you can turn around at any point.

The South Kaibab Trail is a well-maintained dirt trail offering wonderful expansive views of the canyon. This is a great trail for short trips into the canyon of half a day or less. The openness of this trail lends itself to extreme heat during the summer months and little protection from passing storms. The total length is 6 miles roundtrip, but you can turn around at any point. The North Kaibab Trail is the least visited and most difficult of the major inner canyon trails.

The South Rim is the most accessible and a popular destination at Grand Canyon. The South Rim is where you'll find visitor's centers, historical buildings. It has over two dozen viewpoints and trailheads. Because of its popularity, visitors should expect crowds particularly in the busiest seasons, spring, summer, and fall. The North Rim has a shorter season, is harder to get to, is wilder, more secluded and more difficult.

Grandview Point offers an open scenic view of the canyon. This popular viewpoint offers panoramic views of Grand Canyon from east to west, including several bends of the Colorado River. This trail is incredibly steep. In summer, much of the trail is in full sun. In winter, ice and snow make hiking treacherous. Grandview Trail is a rocky trail that leads down into the depths of the Grand Canyon. The trail can be quite rugged, narrow, and steep,

Desert View drive has some scenic views of the Grand Canyon. You can take desert view drive to desert view road and visit the watchtower for some great scenic views. It is a very short walk to the watchtower. Less than a quarter mile walk. It was here that visitors to the canyon in the 1930's could sit in comfort and have outstanding views of the canyon.

Mather Point is a 5 minute walk from the South Rim visitor center, Mather Point is the first view the of Grand Canyon for many people. On a clear day you can see 30 miles to the east and 60 miles to the west. Thanks to it's wide view and the dramatic rock formations, Mather Point is a popular place at Sunrise and Sunset. Be sure to get here early to enjoy the change in colors as the sun rises and sets.

Hopi Point offers panoramic and breathtaking views of the canyon along the scenic Hermit Road. Hopi Point offers five views of the Colorado River. An ideal location at sunrise or sunset. Hopi Point is accessible by the park's free shuttle bus service or a 2.5 mile walk along the Rim Trail. This wooden lookout tower is thought to be the first fire towers in Arizona.

Yaki Point is the only scenic viewpoint on Desert View Drive that is not accessible with a private vehicle. It can be reached using the free Kaibab Rim shuttle, from the Grand Canyon Visitor Center. The view of the canyon opens to the east, with the Desert View Watchtower visible in the distance. A popular view for sunset and sunrise, the lack of private vehicles provides a bit more solitude than other viewpoints.

Cape Royal Drive is a fantastic scenic road leading to various points. Including Walhalla Glades Pueblo, Point Imperial, and Cape Royal. Diverse viewpoints and several trails can be reached via this winding scenic drive that can be a great way to spend anywhere from a few hours to a day exploring the canyon.

The Navajo Bridge is the name of twin steel spandrel arch bridges that cross the Colorado River in the Grand Canyon National Park. Those traveling across the country on Highway 89A between Bitter Springs and Jacob Lake, AZ arrive at two bridges similar in appearance spanning the Colorado River. These two bridges, re one of only seven land crossings of the Colorado River for 750 miles.

East Rim Drive. This section is the only way to drive a car to many viewpoints. It has several viewpoints, where you can stop along the way. The drive is well worth the time for visitors who may not have one or two entire days to visit the Grand Canyon. If you are lucky, you will get to see elk and deer. Watch for elk grazing among the trees, especially south of the road.

Horseshoe bend, the Colorado River created a 1,000-foot deep, 270-degree horseshoe shaped bend in the Glen Canyon. The hike to the overlook is 1.5 miles round-trip over a hardened path. Horseshoe Bend is not part of the United States National Park System. Half of the U-shaped bend is owned by the city of Page, Arizona.

Lipan Point features some of the widest and most expansive canyon views along the South Rim, as well as the longest perspective of the Colorado River. This makes it an ideal spot to enjoy sunrise, sunset, and the night sky. On a clear day, you can see the Vermillion Cliffs 45 miles to the northeast and the curving river to the west as it enters the Inner Gorge of the canyon.

Mohave Point offers excellent views of the Colorado River deep in the canyon below. From here you can also see the Salt Creek, Granite, and Hermit rapids. Another spectacular point for watching the sunset. Mohave Point has a fine view of the near vertical, 3,000-foot-high cliffs. It's located off Hermit road.

Cape Royal and Angel's Window are some of the only spots with views of the Colorado River from the North Rim. From the southeast side of the parking lot, a short wheelchair-accessible path leads to several spectacular viewpoints. The west side of the parking lot is where you can find a picnic area. Roundtrip hiking distance is 0.8 miles.

Powell Point is an overlook along the South Rim of the Grand Canyon. While a fine view of Grand Canyon is visible directly after stepping off the shuttle bus, a short, easy walk along the paved path out to the viewpoint is rewarded with even more excellent views and access to the Powell Memorial.

Toroweap point, also known as Tuweep Overlook a viewpoint of the Grand Canyon. It is in a remote area on the North Rim of the Grand Canyon. The Tuweep area of Grand Canyon National Park is remote and getting there is challenging. There is no water, gas, food, lodging, Wi-Fi, or cell service.

Pima Point is one of the best places on the rim to see, and sometimes hear, the Colorado River. The distant roar of Granite Rapids far below can be heard echoing up the canyon walls on quiet days. Located just before the end destination of West Rim Drive, Pima Point is a great place to stop and take a rest on the way to Hermit's Rest.

An unsigned dirt parking area marks the trail out to Shoshone Point. An easy one-mile walk along an old dirt road takes you through ponderosa forest, which eventually transitions to a juniper woodland near the rim of the canyon. A relatively quiet viewpoint along the rim of the canyon. Shoshone Point is the only area within the park that can be reserved for private events and gatherings.

Hermits Rest is a historic stop off Hermit Road, and the Canyon Rim Trail. It serves as the gateway to magnificent backcountry hiking trails that originate from the Hermit Trail, a steeply winding path into the canyon. Hermit trail offers a wide variety of hiking paths and experiences. This trail is for experienced desert hikers only.

One of the most awesome viewpoints of the Grand Canyon is at Guano Point. It has stunning 360-degree views of the canyon. Guano Point Cafe offers outside seating where you can sit and eat and enjoy the view of the canyon. The West Rim is where you'll find the world-famous Skywalk, Zipline, helicopter tours, scenic viewpoints, shopping and dining.

Grand Canyon Skywalk. Talk about a rush. Walk out on this glass bottom, see through floor structure that you can see awesome views of the Grand Canyon from. This will definitely test your fear of heights. Skywalk gives you the feeling you are walking on air. Skywalk is located at Grand Canyon West's Eagle Point on the Hualapai Reservation and is not affiliated with Grand Canyon National Park.

Things to Do in the Grand Canyon

There's plenty of sightseeing opportunities in the Grand Canyon. But there's also some other fun things to do. Here's some of them.

Visitor Centers are both located on the North and South rim.

Visitor Center Theater. When the visitor center is open, the film, Grand Canyon, a Journey of Wonder, is shown. Admission is free.

Driving. The Canyon Rim Trail continues alongside Hermit Road, a 7-mile scenic road with 9 exceptional overlooks.

Walking, Hiking, Camping. walk part of the well-defined, and mostly level Canyon Rim Trail. Camping is available.

Activities for Kids. Grand Canyon's Junior Ranger program.

Bicycle. You can bring your own bike or rent one.

Guided Learning Adventures. Hiking, Mule Riding, Biking etc.

Mule Trips. 3-hour or overnight trips that travel the canyon rim.

Rafting Trips. Half-day and all-day smooth water trips

Grand Canyon Railway. Take a train ride, check for info.

Helicopter Rides. Take a Helicopter Tour Over the Canyon.

Check Before going. At certain times of the year some parts of the park are not open, and access may change. Reservations may be required.

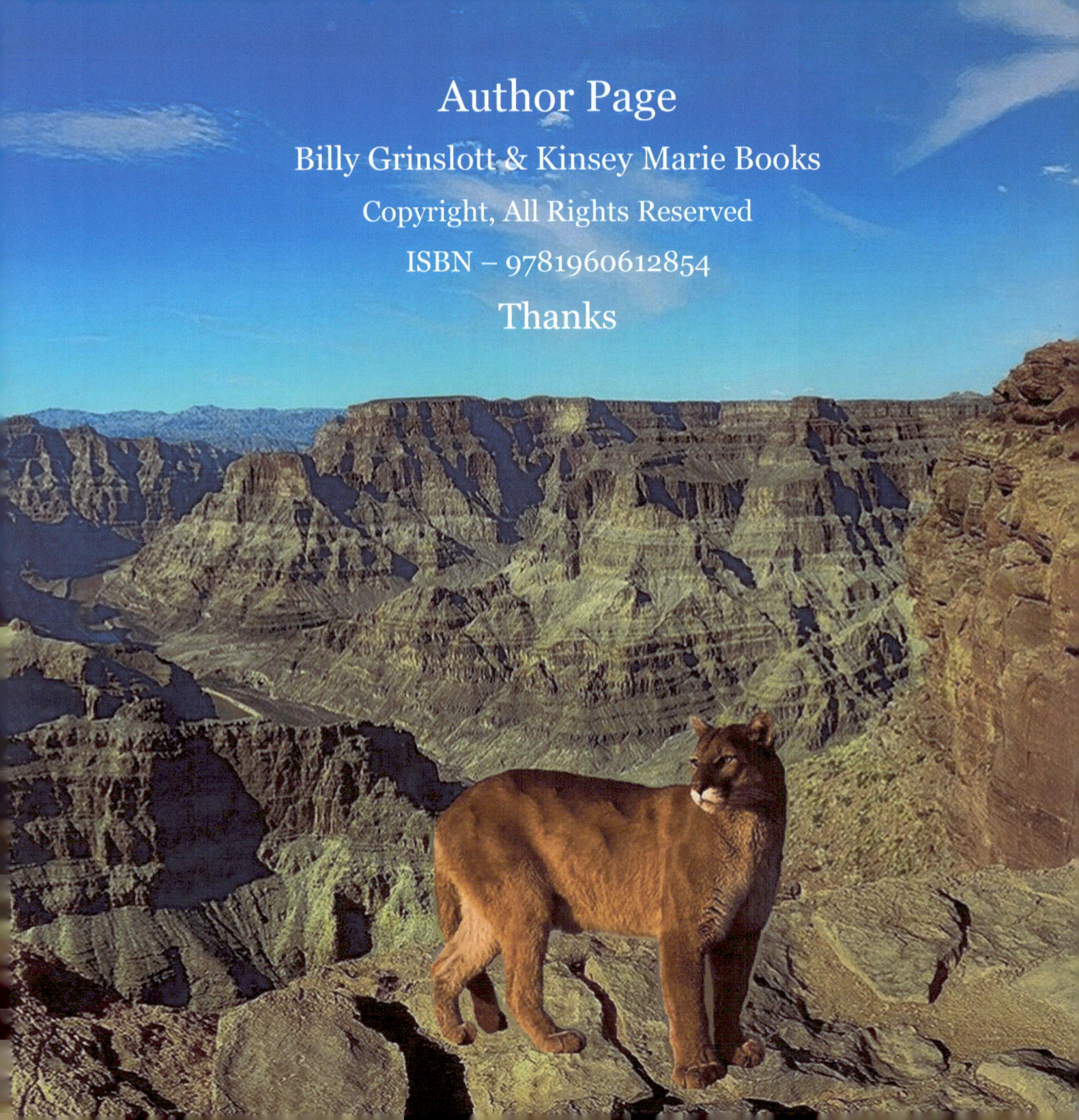

Author Page

Billy Grinslott & Kinsey Marie Books

Copyright, All Rights Reserved

ISBN – 9781960612854

Thanks